AMNESIAC
RADIOHEAD

GUITAR TABLATURE VOCAL

WWW.RADIOHEAD.COM
OR W.A.S.T.E. P.O.BOX 322 OXFORD OX4 1EY

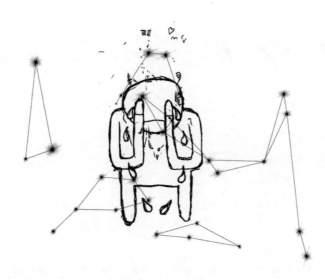

PUBLISHED 2002
© INTERNATIONAL MUSIC PUBLICATIONS LTD
GRIFFIN HOUSE 161 HAMMERSMITH ROAD LONDON W6 8BS ENGLAND

EDITED BY CHRIS HARVEY
DESIGN BY STANLEY & TCHOCK
MUSIC ARRANGED BY ARTEMIS MUSIC LTD

PACKT LIKE SARDINES IN A CRUSHD TIN BOX

Words and Music by Thomas Yorke, Jonathan Greenwood,
Edward O'Brien, Philip Selway and Colin Greenwood

*Key signature denotes D dorian

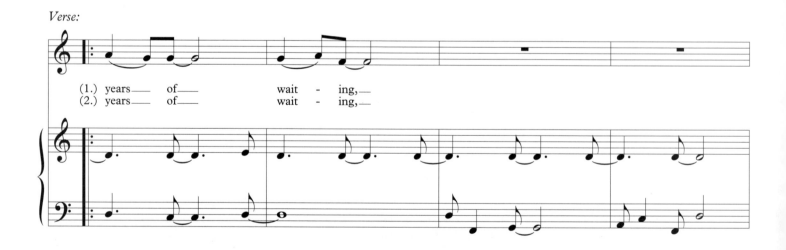

I'm a rea - s'n - 'ble man,— get off— my case,— get off—
I'm a rea - s'n - 'ble man,— get off— my case,— get off—

1.
— my case.—
— my case,— get off.

2.
2. Af - ter — my case.— I'm a rea - s'n - 'ble man,— get off—

— my case,— get off— my case,— get off— my case.

11 bars Synth.+Perc. fx

Af - ter years___ of___ wait - ing.___

I'm a rea - s'n - 'ble man,___ get off___

4 bars Drums+fx

4° w/Gtr. fx

Play 4 times

___ my case,___ get off___ my case,___ get off___ my case.___ (4° tacet) I'm a

5

PYRAMID SONG

Words and Music by Thomas Yorke, Jonathan Greenwood,
Edward O'Brien, Philip Selway and Colin Greenwood

all the fi - gures I used to see.
nothing to fear,___ noth - ing to doubt.___

Ooh,_____ ooh,___

ooh.___

nothing to fear,___ noth - ing to doubt.___

8

There was _____

PULK/PULL REVOLVING DOORS

Words and Music by Thomas Yorke, Jonathan Greenwood,
Edward O'Brien, Philip Selway and Colin Greenwood

1. *Spoken:* There are barn doors
(Verse 3 see block lyric)

2. There are doors that open

by themselves.

and there are revolving doors.
There are sliding doors and there are secret doors.

Doors in the rudders of big ships.   And there are revolving doors.   *Drum loop stops*

cont. sim.

12 bars ad lib. fx

Synth. glissando fx

Repeat to fade

3 bars Drum loop & fx   *fx*

Synth. tape loop

Verse 3:
There are doors that lock
And doors that don't

There are doors that let you in
And out
But never open
But there are trapdoors
That you can't come back from.

YOU AND WHOSE ARMY?

Words and Music by Thomas Yorke, Jonathan Greenwood,
Edward O'Brien, Philip Selway and Colin Greenwood

I MIGHT BE WRONG

Words and Music by Thomas Yorke, Jonathan Greenwood,
Edward O'Brien, Philip Selway and Colin Greenwood

① = E   ④ = D
② = B   ⑤ = A
③ = G   ⑥ = D

sworn   I   saw——   a   light   com-ing   on.——
did   not——   have   you?

(1° only)

I   used to

omit 2°

think,———————   I   used to   think———————

there is   no   fu - ture left——   at   all,——   I   used to——

16

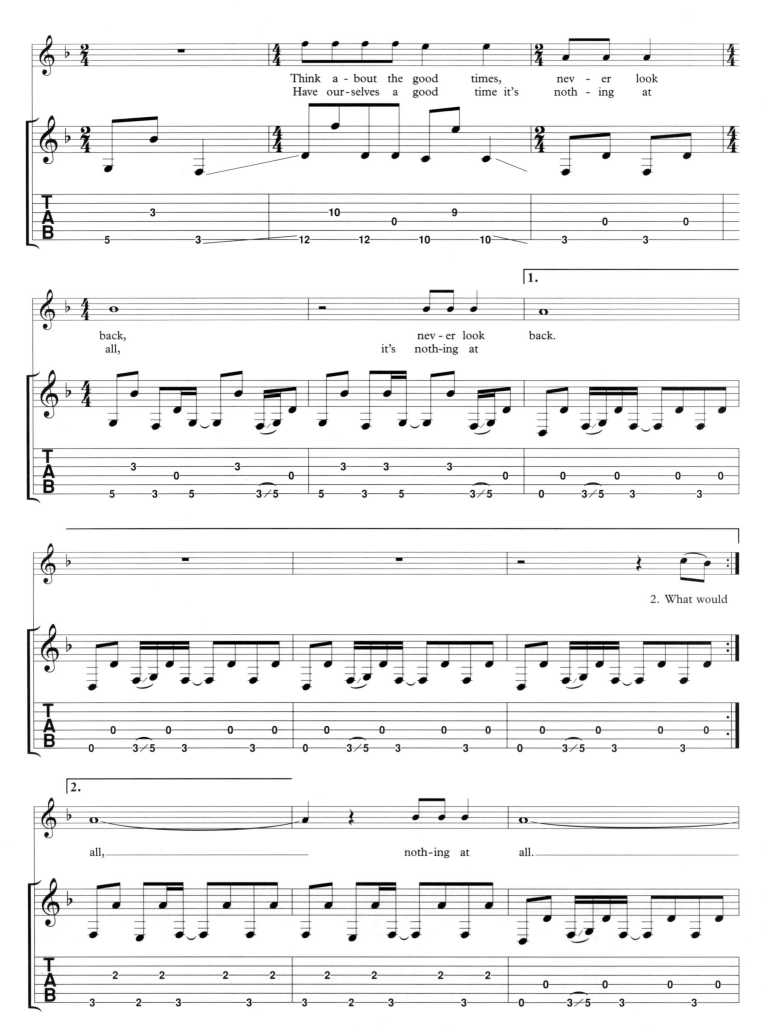

Keep—

it ———
it ———

mov - ing.————
mov - ing.————

1.

2.

Keep— ———

MORNING BELL / AMNESIAC

Words and Music by Thomas Yorke, Jonathan Greenwood,
Edward O'Brien, Philip Selway and Colin Greenwood

Re - lease

me,— re - lease me,— re - lease— me.—

(1° only) Re - lease me.—

KNIVES OUT

Words and Music by Thomas Yorke, Jonathan Greenwood,
Edward O'Brien, Philip Selway and Colin Greenwood

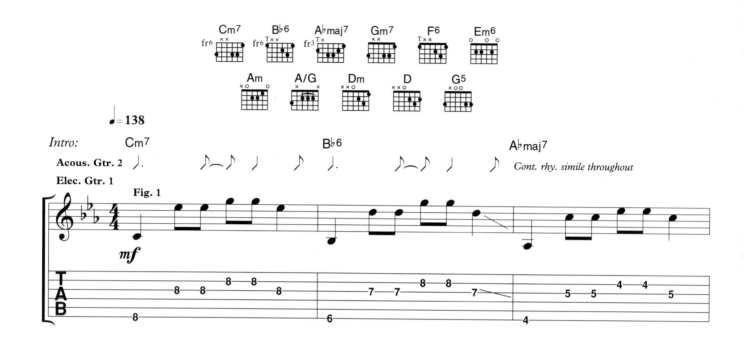

30

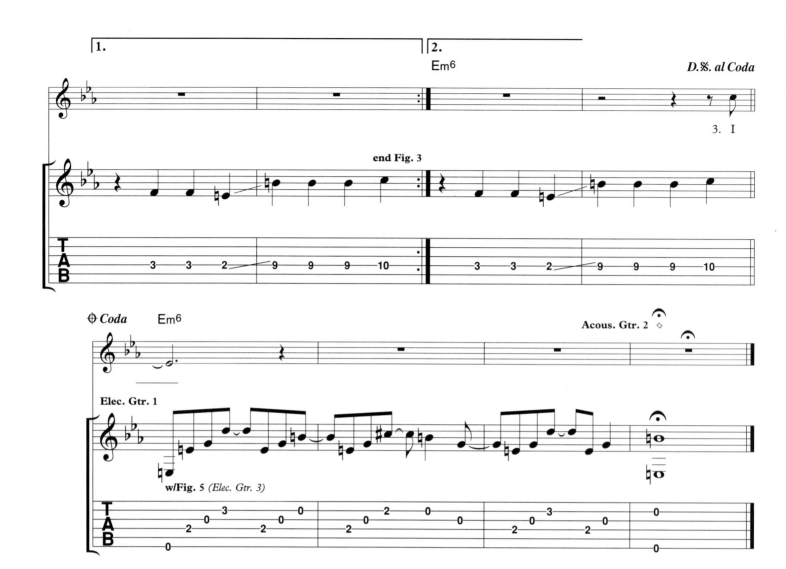

Verse 3:
I want you to know
He's not coming back
He's bloated and frozen
Still there's no point in letting it go to waste.

DOLLARS AND CENTS

Words and Music by Thomas Yorke, Jonathan Greenwood,
Edward O'Brien, Philip Selway and Colin Greenwood

be con - struc - tive.

Bear wit - ness,

we can use,_____

be con-struc-

- - tive

with your blues._

34

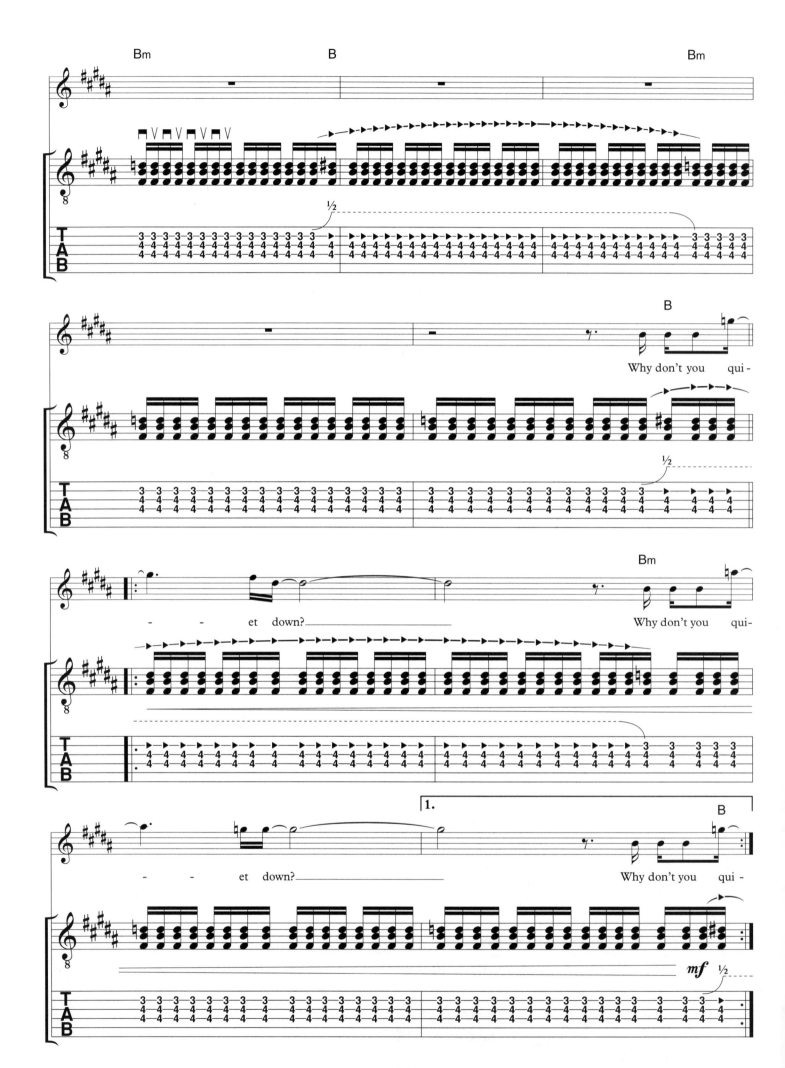

Qui - et down.

You don't live in a bu-si-ness world, you nev-er go out and you nev-er stay in.
We all have goals in a li-be-ral world, liv-ing in times when I can stand it babe.

39

HUNTING BEARS

Words and Music by Thomas Yorke, Jonathan Greenwood,
Edward O'Brien, Philip Selway and Colin Greenwood

LIKE SPINNING PLATES

Words and Music by Thomas Yorke, Jonathan Greenwood,
Edward O'Brien, Philip Selway and Colin Greenwood

I'm liv - ing in cloud cuck - oo —— land.

And this just feels— like —— spin - ning —— plates. ——

My bo - dy's float - ing down a mud - dy ri - ver.

Repeat to fade

sfx

43

LIFE IN A GLASSHOUSE

Words and Music by Thomas Yorke, Jonathan Greenwood,
Edward O'Brien, Philip Selway and Colin Greenwood

sit a-round___ and chat,___ and some-one's list-'ning in.

Well of course I'd like___ to sit a-round___ and chat,___

well of course___ I'd like___ to stay___ and chew___ the fat,___

but of course___ I'd like___ to sit a-round and chat, o-on-ly, on-ly, on-ly,___

46

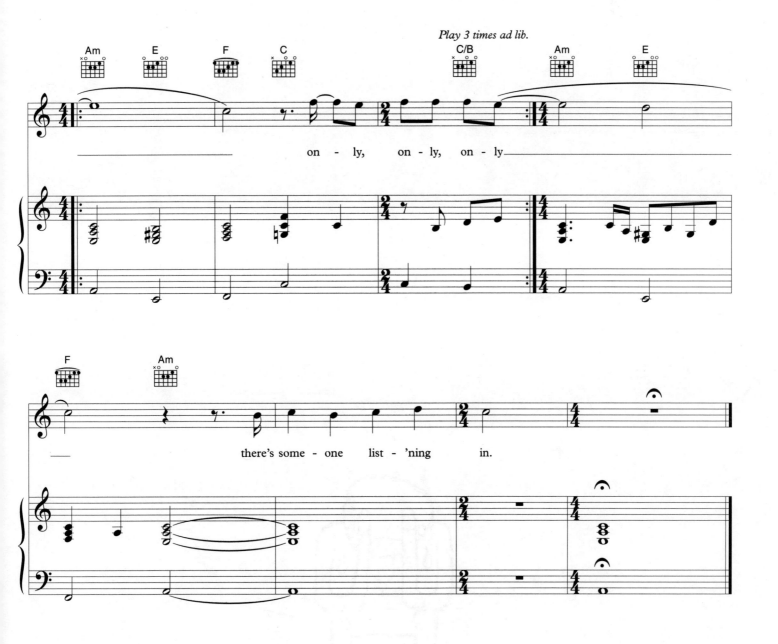

on - ly, on - ly, on - ly

there's some - one list - 'ning in.

Verse 3:
Once again we are hungry for a lynching
That's a strange mistake to make
You should turn the other cheek
Living in a glass house.

Well of course *etc.*

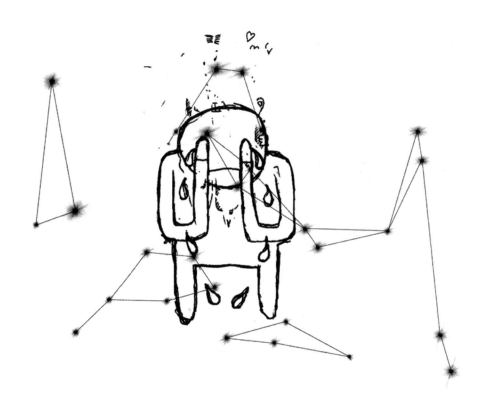